# A TOUCH OF MIDAS

- Poems 1986-2011 -

A Journey Down The Years

# BERNARD M. JACKSON

INDIGO DREAMS PUBLISHING

First Edition: A Touch Of Midas
First published in Great Britain in 2012 by:
Indigo Dreams Publishing,
132 Hinckley Road,
Stoney Stanton
Leics, LE9 4LN
www.indigodreams.co.uk

Bernard M Jackson has asserted his right under the
Copyright, Designs and Patents Act 1988 to be identified as the
author of this work.

©2012 Bernard M Jackson

ISBN 978-1-907401-84-8

British Library Cataloguing in Publication Data. A CIP record for
this book can be obtained from the British Library.

Designed and typeset in Palatino Linotype by Indigo Dreams.
Cover design by Ronnie Goodyer at Indigo Dreams

Printed and bound in Great Britain by Imprint Academic, Exeter

Papers used by Indigo Dreams are recyclable products made from
wood grown in sustainable forests following the guidance of the
Forest Stewardship Council

DON

## ACKNOWLEDGEMENTS

A number of the poems in this collection have previously appeared in such publications as Poetry Now, Reach Poetry, Quantum Leap, The Black Rose, The Dawntreader, Iota, Rhyme Arrival, Poetic Hours, Voice And Verse, Dial 174, Tips Magazine, E—Tips, Poetry Cornwall, Writers' Forum, The Northern Cross,.Rubies In The Darkness, Helicon, Evergreen, This England, Advance, Weyfarers, Poetic Circle Of Friendship, Metverse Muse, Freexpressions, Voice Of Kolkata, Poet, Samvedana, Bridge In Making, Poetcrit, Poetry Monthly, The Wow Factor and in various other publications over the years.

Acknowledgements and thanks are extended to the Editors of these worthy publications, and I am especially grateful to Ronnie Goodyer and Dawn Bauling, joint-editors at IDP, for their constant encouragement and valued assistance in helping to bring this work into being as a collection.

# FOREWORD

The poems in this collection have been written throughout the period of the last twenty five years (1986-2011) and have mostly featured, at some time or other, in small press magazines, international publications and, to some degree, in several of my own thematic collections. Having earlier spent thirty years as a teacher in a number of secondary schools in the North of England, I have long been particularly aware of the imperative requirement that poetry should certainly serve as an essential means of clear communication; and it is precisely with this in mind that the present included poems have variously come into being. Magazine editors, generally, normally expect hopeful poetry submissions to not exceed 30-40 lines in extent, and while this is ever a wise magazine policy, it does necessarily exclude almost any chance of access to writer's longer verse creations. However, a literary cornucopia of the immediate order has happily determined that some of my longer poems shall indeed see the light of day - or, at very least, reach the comforting glow of another person's reading lamp! And incidentally, I make no apologies for resorting to the vernacular in one or two of the present inclusions, for if a poet is to be allowed occasional free rein to his lighter moods, what better excuse could one tender for the introduction of such poems as 'OWLD JEPSON' and 'A PILGRIM STREET BALLAD' ?

My dear friend, fellow poet, editor and publisher, Ronnie Goodyer, at whose gracious behest this collection has been duly assembled, has been the virtual spearhead of the motivation needed to spur this eight-words-a-minute typist into eventual action.

My sincere thanks, then, to Ronnie, and to all those other dedicated editors (past and present) who have so generously assisted the development of BMJ as a writer, by the publication of my work.

*Bernard M Jackson*

# CONTENTS

# A TOUCH OF MIDAS

## - Poems 1986-2011 –
## A Journey Down The Years

# SOMEWHERE

Once upon a time, and cloud-borne
Down skied hope that never yet
Has doused its candled sun,
My dreams still stray;
And in a time where such a day
Has scattered gold on everyone,
Those tousle-heads
Are spreading field for last man in,
Where birdsong pipes from hedge and tree
And where,
From leaning gates and flower-beds,
Men's voices thin upon the air
Re-echo, warm and free;
While early moth and longlegs pass
Across that flattened patch of grass
Where cricket's so intense.
And in this setting still I find
Familiar houses, walls and fence;
And somewhere, where some
Night's aflame,
And in a sense
where time may never leave my mind,
My father calls me,
speaks my name.

## SHADE OF HIS HAND

Slowly, imperceptibly the sky
Emerged from timeless
Settlement.
The Heavens smiled
As clouds ranged high
O'er gilded oceans - whence light brings
Its fleece of gold on angel wings
Through silent, blazed
Infinity.
 - - - But slowly, imperceptibly the sky
Was changing, changing;
Loosening shawls from falls of grey.
 - And night fell fast
As shadows cast
A parody of day.

I thought of childhood's
Cherished skies
 - Now silvern, turning sable!
Cries
Of unseen, sometime birds
Lent memory to fable;
And a wondrous vision
Passed away.
        Canvas of sky!
- O'er light trepanned,
The artist brushed
With Moveless Hand.

# THE PROMISE

Sunlight came
like the unexpected
free-fall of an angel,
and birds
flew in from nowhere wood;
their sudden-fluted canticles
filling out the topmost boughs,
as morning grasped brief fragments of a star.

Splash-dappled from its mainstream,
silver fell to withered leaves
and polished wax of evergreen.
Poor struggled weeds bloomed instantly.
A blousy magpie
swaggered into sight; its shaken halo
giving rise to mid-day's smile,
and blackbirds pottered everywhere.

Then through the brakes
we too
found share of this pervading ecstasy,
entranced by an enormity of light,
a gleam intangible;
its whirl of worlds beyond a world
bold sun had brought to mind;
renewal's metamorphosis
from sylvan death we'd left behind.

# BLACKBIRD

I leaned upon my spade, aware
that he was there;
a most unsettled day, but warm
and drizzle-damp. The sun
emergent, restive
after falls of rain, and I
shirt-sleeved, and up against it in July,
straining at a job half-done.

I saw his dark, blurred
hoppings, heard
the scrape of wood-lath down the fence,
and knew
how through his inching
sidelong down,
he'd amble into view.

Immobility seemed appropriate.
His questing, jetted eyes shone greed;
surprise was not self-evident.
Head-bent, and cocking quick
he eyed me.
- Golden Beak,
work-worn, stained with earth,
divining spade-spent
packages of soil.

I was aware
his stare of button-eye
was fixed on plunder from my toil.
Perhaps with bird-brain acumen,
solution may be found;
a deal we'd strike,
a bargain seal.
and maybe,
if we came to terms,
then he could do the digging,
- - and I'd provide the worms.

# WHERE BLACKBIRD SINGS

The bud has burst full-blown from sleep,
Where half remembered
Shadows creep
Through fern-clad glades and black-thorn,
Deep
In memories that sigh.

The maple, beech and lofty elm
With verdant skeins
Their skies o'erwhelm,
And childhood laughter takes the helm
A host of years,
A thousand years,
So many years gone by.

Beyond the bridge where hedgerows sprawl
And blackbird sings to blackbird's call,
On thorn-scarred knees,
Through thickets,
Crawl
Young dreams that never die.

By foxglove haunt and fern-strewn hill
These childhood wonders
Linger still,
And sunlight strikes my world at will,
A host of years,
A thousand years,
So many years gone by.

# SUNLIT DAYS

I would not trade the gift of Sight
For fame and wealth untold.
- These wondrous eyes more precious are
Than finest crock of gold.
How blest am I by Nature's charm;
To woodland sounds I cling
- where cool winds sigh
Through rustled leaves
And countless songsters sing.

When droplets paint a rainbow dream
And clouds adorn the sky;
When blossoms gleam like royal gems
Where silvan streamlets lie,
I wander through God-given ways
Down paths I surely know,
Through time-appointed sunlit days;

And, in the afterglow,
Where fellowship has traced my course,
As warp and weft entwine,
The darkest night is lit with stars
Whose light is God's design.

For all these gifts, these Earthly joys,
I thank the Lord above;
But treasured more than Time itself,
Is God's greatest Gift of Love.

# A CHILDHOOD ESCAPADE

Sprawling like a severed oak,
Old Jock, the house dog, lay
somnolent on aching paws
through settled spells of day;
by languor seized,
where midge-flies teased
in spirals round his head.
- Dull keeper of a thousand dreams
that circumstance had shed.

My playmates had avoided him,
his owners passed him by
and, like a great unwanted heap,
upon the ground he'd lie
all summer through,
and autumn, too,
a gleam within his eye.

-- A gleam, a dream,
one failing hope!
- I could not leave him so.
        'Come, Jock, to the trees - and play;
        off to the woods we'll go!'

He struggled gamely to his feet,
and followed like a friend
to ramble through that world of green,
where golden sunbeams wend.

We waded through the crystal stream,
we scrambled through the glade,
and out across the sun-scorched fields
to distant hills we strayed
--- till time and hunger fetched us home.

Jock drooped, with listless head.
Our neighbours came to remonstrate:
-'You stole our dog!' they said.

# OWLD JEPSON

No barber ivver tuk ser long
Ter cut a feller's 'air,
Or laiked ser much wi' shavin' soap
Wi t'chap in t'wind-up chair.
Aye, yon wa' fair few year back, nah,
Wi' me nobbut a lad;
Ah went on t'tram bi Beeston 'ill
Ter Jepson's wi' mi Dad.
Why Dad went there ah'll nivver knaw
(Ner neether did mi Mam).
T'only gud abaht it wa
We allus went bi tram.

Owld Jepson wor-a fussy chap,
Bald 'ead an wrinkled skin;
'is glasses sumwheer dahn is nawse,
'is little 'ead reight thin.
'e bustled rahnd an'buzzed n'ummed;
It wor-an orful noise;
Well, right enuff fer dozy men,
But nowt fer little boys.

'is shop wa' panelled out wi' wud,
Reight owld it wor-an all.
Yer sat aroun' all Saturday
Jus waitin' fer yer call.
An't sem owld gaffers kem each week,
(Ah'd think theer waitin' yet)
Fer t'chance o'gettin Back n' Sides

Afower they edd a bet.
Well, sumtimes when 'e 'ad a bloke
Orl lathered in 'is chair,
'e'd up an 'tek dahn t'bunch o'keys,
Mek-on 'e were not theer,
An' toddle off dahn t'reight owld street
('is calls o'nature fer ter meet).

But t'other fellers, sat aroun',
Di'n't seem too bothered though.
They scanned 'is las' week's Yorkshire Posts
An' med ther nawses blow.
Each bloke wore greasy overalls,
A flat cap on 'is 'ead:
While sum 'ad brought ther bait wi' em,
Tomaters, slabs o'bread.
An theer we sat, me an' mi Dad,
Jus' waitin' ter be dun,
While Jepson wound 'is gramophone
Fer Gracie Fields an' fun.

# GRANDFATHER

No more impressive than the rest,
his downstairs flat
yawned out across a dog-patch;
a place, at least, in which to live,
where dark-green, metal window-frames
squared corporate conformity.

Tainted by past usage,
time turned brown
light-papered walls
and mishmash palls of furnishings.
Stale smell of soup addressed the breath
of reeky pipes and polish tins,
while papers, tools and bits and bobs
were scatterered where he'd find them.

But ram-rod straight - and come what may,
Grandfather's clock marched down the day
Tick-tock, tick-tocking
Time away.

The family portrait gazing down
smiled Nineteen-Twelve, and he,
resplendent in red uniform,
the steadfast soul of gallantry;
with black moustache and head a-tilt.

-   A soldier to the very hilt!

I'd asked him once if he would say
how it had been,
so long ago - so far away -
and he a soldier of the Queen;
but when at last he'd raised his head,
considering the words I'd said,
he reached for his tobacco jar

- and gazed out into India.

# FEARNVILLE SONNET

The same clouds sail that great expanse of sky,
And old winds gust remembered brakes of trees,
Where birdsong pipes its agelong melodies
Around young dreams, in thickets where I'd lie;
For, as winged years have spread, so did they fly,
Yet live must they, in all my memories.
The seasons turn, but time shall not harm these
Childhood moments caught upon a sigh.

Beyond THE NOOK, the little woodland glade
Will long bloom free, though years shall come to pass,
And winds shall stir those boughs, each blade of grass,
Each leafy den where childhood's shadow strayed.
Though time may dim the vision, who can tell
How dreams might kindle days we knew so well.

# SING A NEW SONG

My grandfather, when old and grey,
still carried with him everywhere
the regimental, silver-topped stick
of a company sergeant-major,
for this he'd borne through India.

And childhood whims sought postage stamps
and picture books - with Robert Clive,
bold elephants, and old bazaars;
where minarets in templed towns,
and the broad, free-flowing
sacred streams
of a world, so far from all I'd known,
brought vivid scenes of India.

Then schooldays issued well-thumbed books
that sketched out Ghats
and coastal plains;
with monsoons inking arrowed maps
- and bar-graphs, charts and humdrum spells,
as we dissected India.

But the more I learnt, the less I knew,
until I found enlightenment;
for in these daunting latter days,
within a land we once had ruled,
there spreads in peace and fellowship
a new hope born of India.

# FARMS OF LONG AGO

In time-forgotten coombs and dells
Where cottages lay sleeping,
And half a hundred hedgerows
Sprawled down muddy tumbled lanes,
Where soughing breeze brought steeple bells,
Their ageless vigil keeping,
And birdsong from the coppice
Echoed woodland-sweet refrains,
The farmer ploughed with faithful team
And set his stock to grazing;
His sheep roamed o'er the hillside,
And his hireling pitched the hay.
The farmer's wife would share his dreams
Beside the hearth a-blazing,
When final tasks were ended
In the old, time-honoured way.

But horse and plough are far and few
 - The farmstead is no longer;
The hen-run by the five-barred gate
May now be seen no more;
For those once-familiar faces,
Seen in England's country places,
Have been buried with their grandsires
In a world that passed before.

# BALLADE

Those sunscaped dreams have sadly passed away,
enraptured vision now no longer dwells
where freedom reigned in carefree childhood's day,
nor knows what fate or fortune time fortells.
The wild wood, blue with sheen of nodding bells,
the wanton brook we waded from first-spring,
we once had thought were lasting sylvan spells.
Where is the joy that such thoughts bring?

In moments with once bosom friends at play,
so fleet of foot, and bounding like gazelles,
we traced the path of each forgotten way,
through seasoned swards and golden asphodels.
Where instant charm from sunlight, time compels.
How blithely, then would hidden blackbirds sing!
From vanquished trees their song no longer swells.
Where is the joy that such thoughts bring?

Remembered shades are but a roundelay,
swift fragrance that some passing mood impels,
whose measured earthly cost must long outweigh
the worth of gorse and scarlet pimpernels;
for hoary time soon sounds its fateful knells,
and lingered leaves to autumn boughs then cling.
Thus, changing phase our late rememberence quells!
Where is the joy that such thoughts bring?

In fading years, cold sentiment dispels,
though some might ever crave that final fling.
Time's childhood dreams bequeath but empty shells;
Where is the joy that such thoughts bring?

## SONNET - LASTING SONG

How fickle is the accolade of fame,
Time's withered bay bestowed on poets few,
Whose glory is dependent on a name,
That gifted verse might gain its Earthly due.
How soon ambition fails each cherished hope,
Till dreams on waxen wings no more may fly;
No more to find full measure of their scope,
For praise, like leaves of chance, shall pass them by.

And yet, to scale those heights, to rise in song,
To know beyond belief this soul is free,
Is greater far than favour with that throng
Who'd love some name, though scorn rare poesy,
      - Give king his crown, and moment's man his say,
        But sing my soul, forever and a day.

# CHAFFINCH

Gold of sunlight caught him;
Wrought into a multicoloured show
His fine display of featherings.
Some random flight between the trees
Had brought him there,
And spring's bells on the balming air of morning
Had discovered him:
His tripping, metalled melody
A pink-pink share of eloquence
That fringe of woodland brings.
    Brief troubadour aflame with joy;
    A jester on the brink of song.


    But given, not for long,
To sharp, incautious vanity,
The chaffinch - too fluffed up to fear,
And heeding stealthy watchers near,
Remained to be admired.
Then,
    Look at me! Oh, look at me!
(His pink, his green, his slate-blue crown.)
Pink,
Pink again;
A searing blur of spectrum, down
Through stilly air
Till, calm on wings from rustled boughs,
    He settled like a prayer.

# KINGFISHER

Killer of fish,
A fire-burst, fleeting
Cobalt blur on restless air,
A day-blest iridescence, where
From sapphire haze
He'll stake his claim.

In fulsome leaves of boughs
He'll pause,
With questing beak
And thin, red claws,
Till glance of stream
Rare chance allows.

Then down and down
He'll strike to find
A sparkled flash of quick-finned prey

- - - But Halcyon has gone his way.
No more the fisher in the Dene,
Sheer beauty that was sometimes seen
In woodland, where
Bright leaves make play.
To fading dreams his flight's consigned.
  - His world belongs to yesterday.

# THOMAS BEWICK

All country things he loved.
Down woodcut lanes
he'd etched from Time,
through shades of graven memory,
he scraped young days from Cherryburn

- - - till makeshift road,
hedge-bordered field,
the cottage and the cluttered farm
Were whittled to an artist's whim.

No lowly task he undertook
that showed no spark of genius;
his hand upon the moment's blade
winged birds, carved trees,
made vignettes loom; and from that dream,
with facets of stilled circumstance,
immortalised a rustic world,
combining skill of master-craft
with sense of rural
          symmetry.

# CAWOOD CASTLE

Though time and tangled intrigue have laid waste
To buttressed walls of Cawood's stately pile,
Some remnant of past splendour may be traced, -
long-spared by chance that let not War defile
This lofty Gatehouse - All that now remains
Of what was once a palace graced by kings;
Where prelates dwelt, who feasted royal trains
With pageantry and all that power brings.

Here fortune smiled and barons quaffed fine ales,
And York was but a carriage-ride away.
As age succeeded age, on higher scale,
Episcopal magnificence held sway;
Till Nevilles failed and Wolsey lost his charm.
 - Now Cawood gapes - - - time's entrance to a farm.

# THAT FAIRGROUND GLOW

From fading winter, year by year,
With accent strange and swarthy tan,
Those fairground folk would soon appear.
 - Their cables coiled round caravan,
As sheet by sheet broad canvas spread
In hues of blues, greens, yellows - - red.
Bold youngsters flocked from near and far
To drive the dashing dodgem-car;
And lounged like lords on shilling rides,
Or jostled crowds past painted sides
Of garish stalls where fun and laughter,
Mixed with cries, long-echoed after.

- - - Pennies rolled like quickened rain,
And rifles cracked - - again, again
From tented booths, whilst everywhere
Bright sing-song music filled the air,
Together with the barker's cries
 - "Come, ring a bowl and win a prize!"
In misting nights of pitch and toss,
And fairy-lights and candy-floss,
Where boy met girl - - and time brought gleam
Of fairground glow - - to fancy's dream.

# GEORGE LEWIS - NEW ORLEANS JAZZ MUSICIAN

Some late sequestered night I'll seek again
Lost moments of my youth where time ran wild
Across remembered years, when charm beguiled
With dancing rhythm beating ceaseless strain;
And syncopate in fancy, I'll remain
To dwell within some place where music, styled
In matchless, simple freedom, undefiled,
Pulsates its cadenced, improvised refrain.

For never was there rhapsody so rare
As when this minstrel piped, with favoured few,
Those silvern sounds, to charm the settled air
Like falling rain that glistens Earth anew.
 - So steadfast stands the man who'd bravely dare
Transform his world from ebony to blue.

# OVER THE TOP

From Huddersfield, the road curls high,
Till bristled moorland meets the sky,
And half-seen hamlets time defy
In coombs of distant yesterday.

Past Slaithwaite, up to Floating Lights,
By dry-walled stone and fogging heights,
Through wind-blown days
And rain-swept nights.

It seems like only yesterday,
When week-ends brought me back to Camp
 - A soldier braving cold and damp
And hitching lorries on the way.

It might have been but yesterday:
 - Past Diggle and, should time allow,
Along that stretch to Mossley Brow.
Though years have flown, I see it now
Down roads that lead to yesterday.

# NIGHT SHADES

Late
breezes
Sweep the street
as leaves of chance
make haste to greet the night in autumn's dance;
and half-glimpsed wakeful clouds are hurried by
through canvas heights
where lost dreams
hidden
lie.
Moon
makes ghosts
of shadows
and stark trees sway,
though branches had been still as death, by day.
From out of nowhere, springs a slithered flight
of velvet jet
to forage
jungle
night.

# SUNLIT LEAVES

When westward sinks the sun, tall trees espouse
Immensity of light, where all's aglow
Within a world at peace. Slow waters flow
Through silent sylvan ways, as time allows
Stilled magic to the Dene. From heightened boughs
The blackbird sings; and folk who pass below
Find rapture of the verdure's constant show
In moments that a summer's day endows.

Eternal is the flame that ne'er consumes,
Yet blazons leaves; nor shall one instant fade
From woodland reign that readily assumes
This seasoned garb, immortally arrayed.
In traceries where sunlight shines between,
God's glory is a miracle of green.

# TO A HIDDEN BIRD

It seemed as if a thousand sparks enflamed
An interlacing canopy of green,
Till gold and silver glittered strands were seen
In tapestry that sunlight had proclaimed;
Then softly, though by quietude untamed,
Where brightest leaves shone glory in the Dene,
Cascades of rippled music came between
Untrodden groves, from singer yet unnamed.

For out of flame, there sang the hidden bird,
A plaintive minstrel, piping through the boughs
With more than normal eloquence allows;
So beautiful a song I'd seldom heard.
My soul was charmed by this most welcome host,
But nowhere could I trace the moment's ghost.

# NEWCASTLE SONNET

Upon these strands the river-city sprawls,
A sleeping titan, pitched against the sky
Athwart a dream, whose memory recalls
Great sailing-ships and coaly days gone by.
On burly banks the builder plied his skill,
Where warren streets down-wind their dusty ways,
And leaning homes of merchant-men are still
Resplendent in facades of former days.

This is the town I love, an urbane soul
Imbued with wit and canny northern pride,
Where yet the knell of circumstance must toll
On falling trades and craftsmen, known worldwide.
A stranger in their midst, a pulse is mine
To beat within this heartland of the Tyne.

# JESMOND DENE - NEWCASTLE UPON TYNE

Late glory, spreading fleece of embered sky,
Lit wide Earth's western veils with crimson glow
Beyond cloud-glittered islands - - while, below,
A woodland benediction made reply,
Till all the Dene was filled with firefly
Of diamond-sparkled leaves, in silvan show
Where sanctity of sunlight would bestow
That final grace - for evening was nigh.

And yet we felt some strange surpassing sense
That witnessed wonders stay, though seem to fade.
What artist would consign such craft immense
To nothingness, where most his soul had strayed?
 - This matchless charm that stills when sun has set,
Nor God, nor Man, nor shall then Time forget.

# NIGHT-WALK

Twelve o'clock,
a cold cloak clinging
dampness on the late-night air;
the calm vault singing
silent bells, and everywhere
a myriad cascade of gems
to keep ablaze their night with stars.

Cold midnight,
and, while Jesmond sleeps,
the street lamp's amber
stains that storeyed tower,
and the paned and pin-pricked
worlds from curtain peeping,
half-detached and out of sight.

 - A witching hour!
My footsteps treading
sanded sounds by gravelled ways,
as through the night
a house-dog barks
ambivalence, that strays
quick-slinking fur from hunting-grounds;

While, out of dark eternity,
the season's cold nocturnal things
have battened down their savage wings
to hoot their age-long
anguish in the park.

# BARN OWL

Straining half-light down the thread
Of night's slow-creeping thoroughfare,
From fluffed-up brown
His dark-eyed stare
Must watch, must wait;
His silvered face
A heart beneath a hunter's moon.

Yet, somewhat soon, from disused shed
He'll kill for kindred;
Float his silent, mottled spread,
His hook-nosed whispers
Down skimmed fields;
A velvet felon, claws to clutch
Whence Nature yields
Nocturnal boon some quest has stirred.

And mouse and vole,
Or small wild fowl,
Or unsuspecting little bird,
Will tumble prey to taloned falls
of sometimes seen, though seldom heard
 - - Barn Owl.

# SONNET - THE OLD SHRINE

Stray light may chance upon it in the glade:
this unpretentious, ruined heap of stone,
Whose hooded pilgrims, bowed in penance, prayed
Till time, the seasoned caller, claimed its own.
No door or glass may shutter this retreat,
Nor is there roof to shelter it from rains;
Around rough walls the gusty showers beat,
And songbirds sing their age-old sweet refrains.

Yet broken stones may harbour inner peace,
For strollers still bestow upon this bower
Faith's passing glance, and gifts that never cease.
 - A cross of twigs, a solitary flower.
Then long may Sun its golden strands entwine
The gracious boughs that overhang this shrine.

# BALLAD FOR A TALL SHIP

There's a stir along the wharfside,
For a ship is on the way,
And a crowding swell is swarming by the Quay;
And it's not your twenty-tonner
That the people prize today,
But a tall three-master, trimmed and running free.

> CHORUS
> And it's Oh, to ride the breakers
> On the rolling distant foam,
> And we'll wish to God that we could go to sea,
> With a roaring wind to take us
> Oh, so very far from home;
> - Aye, it's seaward bound that I wish to be.

For she's out upon the Briny
With a square-rigged fore and main,
Stretching topsails stitched in canvas to the sky.
And it's not your thirty gunner,
Or a galleon from Spain,
But the empress of an ocean, passing by.

> CHORUS
> And it's Oh, to ride the breakers
> On the rolling distant foam,
> And we'll wish to God that we could go to sea,
> With a roaring wind to take us
> Oh, so very far from home;
> - Aye, it's seaward bound that I wish to be.

Soon she'll glide the murky river,
Like the sailing ships of yore,
And so many folk will swell the banks to see
How this proud-rigged vessel made it
From her distant foreign shore,
As she rides the falling billows on the lee.

       CHORUS
       And it's Oh, to ride the breakers
       On the rolling distant foam,
       And we'll wish to God that we could go to sea,
       With a roaring wind to take us
       Oh, so very far from home;
       - Aye, it's seaward bound that I wish to be.

Aye, she'll berth there by the Quayside
On the canny banks o'Tyne,
And they'll deck her out with bunting, flags an' all;
Then we'll cheer the folk who man her
       - with a final cheer that's mine,
For those grand old ships that face the ocean's squall.

       CHORUS
       And it's Oh, to ride the breakers
       On the rolling distant foam,
       And we'll wish to God that we could go to sea,
       With a roaring wind to take us
       Oh, so very far from home;
       - Aye, it's seaward bound that I wish to be.

# PARSON WOODFORDE

Parson Woodforde long preserved
Warm vignettes of his treasured
World. -
Plain workaday of rustic folk.
And flight of feathered pen
Unfurled
The cattle field and furrowed loam
As he from gentle stirrings spoke
From very heart about his home.

This Norfolk parson, Godly man,
Was loved by servant, colleague, friend;
His journal was his
Masterplan,
A wondrous world he might extend.
From diaried spell, brief glimpses bring
Rich counterpane of woods and farm,
The market-township and the charm
Of scattered cotts; while on the wing,
The many season-patterned birds.

Here lived the parson.
Chosen words
Have measured out a life sublime -
He wears his cloth with dignity
In chronicles of time.

# NORHAM CASTLE

On crumbled knolls, above the swollen Tweed,
Bold Norham stands, a rampart from the last
Brief glimpse of Marmion, its ramparts past
Their usefulness. In former times of need,
From arrow-loops, great sandstone walls brought speed
Of flinted combat, as each deadly blast
Repelled the storm of border; archers fast
With raining crossbows, equal to the deed.

Though motte and bailey still grace rising ground,
Cold silence buries bitterness and pain,
Save where the swallows flit with wind-swept sound
Like errant arrows darting once again.
This sun-kissed ruin, set upon a hill,
Has long-survived the men who came to kill.

# ENGLAND EXPECTS

Where the old Cinque Ports are sleeping
In a world that used to be,
Whose churches and great castles grace the land,
Where the village bells are keeping faith
With time and constancy;
Where towns that were old England
Proudly stand;

Where the fields and farms and hedgerows
Bring a glimpse of life before;
Where woodlands trace the haunts of hunted kings;
Where the mallard wings, and sedge grows;
Where the cities still restore
Green parklands to their glory;

Where there sings
An anthem for remembrance
Of the nation that we were,
And the destiny we know we might have seen,
There's a spirit that is England,
There's a movement, there's a stir
Within all loyal hearts.
 - God save the Queen!

# A DREAM WE MIGHT SHARE

When the pageant is spent
And the legend's no more,
And the might that was British
No pride may restore,
Will the few that revere Her
Take heart and proclaim,
From the shores of remembrance,
Her glorious fame?

Will the old flag be cherished,
Shall Freedom be praised
By the sons of the sons
Of the heroes She's raised?
Will the daughters of daughters
Bring joy to their young,
With the songs that
The mothers of mothers have sung?

In a world of Tomorrow
Will Her children attest
To a nation's achievements;
Shall Britain be blest?

Oh, waste not the moment,
Give madness no claim;
Though we may stand alone,
We must yet praise Her name.
Let the bells peal for Freedom
That faith may restore
A dream we might share
- - - Till the anthem's no more.

# THE LADY OF THE LAKE

In a moment born of stillness,
Where rare majesty of light
Gleams upon enchanted waters
Seldom glimpsed by mortal sight,
There, beyond a mystic valley,
Whose fresh morning is awake,
In an aura of charmed beauty
Dwells the Lady of the Lake.

Here, the green grass glows like emeralds,
Gracing bloom of every hue
Round the fringes of the Lakeside,
As the early morning dew
Bedecks all leaves with opals,
While the swan and wild sheldrake
Wait like ghosts within the shallows
For the Lady of the Lake.

And the skies, so blue around her,
Match her lustrous silken gown,
While stray sunbeams weave through tresses
Of fine burnished hair swept down;
And her dark eyes sparkle rapture
That no instant might forsake,
As she walks upon the waters.
 - Lovely Lady of the Lake.

Oh, a hundred hidden angels
Voice with gladness at her tread,

And her golden girdle glistens
As through light she strides ahead,
Whilst emergent from those waters,
Lo, an arm, that Man might take
Excalibur, long-promised
by the Lady of the Lake.

# THE PASSING OF THE GRAIL

From dark shades of a castle's gloom,
By some great timeless force,
Cold grey-stone portals burst with light,
Celestial its source;
A light so pure, so mystical
That those within the hall,
Proud knights and ladies, banqueting,
Were paralysed, withal.

And silent as the grave, there came
A strange and daunting sight,
Four slender vestal virgin maids
Arrayed in gowns of white.
Aloft, one bore an ancient spear
That gleamed with sacred gore;
Another raised a candled stem,
Ethereal, by the door.

A third maid clasped a silvern dish,
As through the hall they passed,
Fair cortege of the Holy Grail.
 - The guests were all aghast,
For Blanchefleur, Lady of renown,
A chalice held on high,
That those who yet were pure of heart
Adored, as she passed by.

Then Galahad, Grail's chosen knight,
Arose as in a dream;
To end of quest he stumbled forth,
His widened eyes agleam,
As, drawing on his noble sword,
Blade-down, a cross he raised,
And thus he joined the hallowed train
Whereon those there had gazed.

With vestal maids, bold Galahad
Now passed beyond recall,
Beyond the silence of the night
That stilled a banquet hall.

# ONE MORE TIME

When Basie played
and swayed, bright chords
swept fire from his fingertips,
and the Kid from Redbank
rolled and riffed
while spotlights glittered tenors.

His piano charmed with measured stride;
and, driven by pulsating bass,
ensemble burst with baritone,
till horns raised golden splendour.

Then, out of coda came the flute
through babbled stream of microphone;
twisting, turning, bending notes
as Frank Wess played the piper.

When Basie flashed expansive smile
to orchestrate immensity,
his sideman found ecstatic heights.
        "Just Swing!" some said
        "just Kansas-style!"

 - - - But Basie's call for
"One more time!"
confirmed his lasting
        legend.

# SANDSTONE

Sandstone island,
Sandstone shore,
High tide, low tide;
Breakers' roar,
Crafting sandstone's
Crag-caped land,
Strewn with boulders,
Sand on sand.

Surf-hewn, time-hewn,
Lined and edged,
Sea-shaped, wind-scaled,
Carved and ledged,
Age-old sandstone,
Sandstone rock;
Sandstone keepers, sandstone stock.

Sandstone raised the lighthouse lure;
Island light will never more,
Never more
Leap through the night
From granite's eye
On sandstone site.

Sandstone island,
Rock-strewn land,
Sandstone, sandstone
 - Sand on sand.

## STORM PETREL

Wilting sea-bird, wing-flung mite,
a trough-bound, ragbag of the sea,
his flight is found in wake of ships,
but salt-flashed,
free.
Hypnotic ripples draw down,
flip him
wraithlike from his turmoiled sky;
his leeward-limping
clasping foam
of seething cauldrons, heaving high
where mariners so far from home
still mark his moods.

- They know him well!
Before full fury of the storm,
he pressages an ocean's swell.

# KIRKSTALL ABBEY

Grey stone, cold and crumbling,
A powerhouse of prayer,
Raised by monk and mason,
Where the ribbon of the Aire
Thrice-blessed the soil of Seleth
And the souls that chanced his way,
Now keeping watchful hours
In a world beyond its day.

Endowed by pledge of baron,
To be built at his behest,
This God-blest pile gave skills their toil
And travellers their rest;
The poor, the sick, the hunted folk
Found haven there, and peace,
Where shadowed stalls within grey walls
Raised plainsong without cease.

No sign of monk and mason, now,
Or farm-hands tending sheep;
No fisherfolk, no weavers,
Or beadsmen who might keep
A constant share of fervent prayer.
And plainsong's heard no more,
For Kirkstall's but a ruined shell
That time will not restore.

# HOME FROM THE SEA

My grandmother's grandfather, hoary and lean,
Had captained a vessel,
A fine brigantine,
A merchant-ship rigged to her top-gallant sail,
And bound for deep waters.
  - Aye, many's the tale
He would tell to that small child
Who climbed on his knee,
- - - My grandmother's grandfather, home from the sea.

From slow hush of evening,he'd heave a great sigh
For the salt-spray, the swell and the lone seabird's cry,
As, like wind in the mizzen,
He'd soundly relate
How they'd crossed the great oceans;
- - And tell of their fate
In the storms that lashed madly
On mountains of waves,
And of deck-hands swept down
To those watery graves;

How dolphins came sporting, when all was at peace;
How the calm lapping waters
Gave seamen release
From the rigours of rigging and hoisting a sail;
When a pipe of good baccy
And an old seaman's tale
Brought laughter and fiddling, and comradeship too.
But sadly those vessels had dwindled to few,
- - And command but a fading dream.

     - Lonesome was he,
     My grandmother's grandfather - - home from sea.

# KYRIELLE

Down distant shades I've shed my dreams,
Have cast aside Ambition's schemes.
This world has turned before my gaze,
For life is but a passing phase.

Fine friendships, fostered long ago,
And fleeting charms I used to know,
Have cloudlike drifted down the days,
For life is but a passing phase.

What profit could it be to Man
To gain the world? - Beyond this span,
No treasure of the moment stays,
For life is but a passing phase.

Then must I strive for better things,
Seek solace where the songbird sings,
For Time all earthly joy outweighs,
And life is but a passing phase.

# A TOUCH OF MIDAS

Rising glow of neon
balms the backs of motorways,
cascading careless
coffers into night.
Down dark parades the traffic roars,
while
somnolent by measured shores,
where falls of satin,
sudden, gaudy,
curtain all suburbia,
cold time creeps on.

- - With a just-like-that,
an old black cat
slips deep into oblivion
as, somewhere
in a sidelong street,
the icy edge of ten-o-clock
nips at the fingertips of winter,
leaps
glistened roofs,
whose glaze stray moonbeams hold,
then out across wet walkways
where
the neon spreads its gold.

# DOWN, DOWN TO ROMNEY TOWN

Out of the mists of awakening time,
The bells of St. Nicholas solemnly chime,
From a dream lost in legend
Where old worlds belong,
In the echoing strains
Of a slow carillon.

And it's Down, down
To Romney Town,
With a string of grey ponies to meet you;
Aye, Down, down
To Romney Town,
And there's gentlemen there who will greet you
With many a tale
Of a life under sail,
And the perils that brought you their booty,
Till swift as the night
They will vanish from sight.
        - And to Hell with the Revenue duty!

To the fair we will go,
Where they'll dance heel and toe,
As the fiddle goes spinning and reeling.
There'll be laughter and song
From a gathering throng;
And the travellers wheeling and dealing!

Aye, wheeling and dealing, and dicing their day
In their low-raftered taverns
With stone walls so grey,
While the womenfolk gossip
And youngsters make play,
Dancing heel and toe down at the fair.

And it's Down, down
To Romney Town,
Where the Redcoats are drinking their Rhenish;
Aye, Down, down to Romney Town,
For the master has stock to replenish.

There's a mist on the Marsh
And a tang from the sea;
And a ship lies at anchor
Where the shallows run free.
There'll be lace for my lady,
- - - Some token for me,
When we whistle a tune
At the fair-oh!

And it's Down, down
To Romney Town;
Keep a watch
For there's muskets for priming;
Aye, Down, down to Romney Town,
        St. Nicholas Bells
                        - - slowly chiming.

## THE SPLINTERED DRUM

Out of fallen night's entrenchment,
Execration and the mud,
From the manning of their fox-holes
Swelling shadows in the wood,
Whence all life was on a knife-edge,
Loyal duty but a joke,
Battle-torn, the brave battalion
Through the fields of Flanders broke.

Out of slime and stench they stumbled
With their wounded, each platoon
Watchful where the great guns rumbled
Beneath a scarred and angry moon.
For soon upon the blinding onset
Of grim nightfall's cold attack
They rose in tattered tens and hundreds,
And no soldier there held back.

How they fell is half-remembered,
How they fought is little known,
In young flowerings of manhood
Where one bitter truth was sown.
Yet my kinsman was among them;
There he died.  One sudden flame
Has left him there among the fallen;
Fallen kinsman with my name.

Often have I tried to reach him,
Labouring poetic sighs;
Formed the sketch work, drawn upon it,
Daunted by Death's darkened skies,
Where, beyond the boom of glory,
Felled from England's martial show,
Drummer Rowley dreams of Erin
And the land he used to know.

# THE HERITAGE

And was it, then, from faded sounds
o'er moss-spread, undulating mounds,
that raised their cold
remembrance
from the ruined stones of Time;
or was it from some might-have-been
we'd sensed the martial glory
of an empire past its prime
   - timeless as the curlew's call?
- - You know this was not all,
for did we not then feel
lost moments shared together,
quickening a glint of steel
and booted scrape of leather
on the Wall,
as out of clambered images
emergent sunlight made that leap
to martial ranks of Romans,
from the settled world we keep?

# WHERE CALMNESS REIGNS - TO R.T. (R.I.P)

Now fades the folding night.  A dawning gleam
Brings brightness far beyond Life's watchful shores;
And timelessness emerges from a dream,
As rhapsody a brighter hope restores,
Somewhere close to Avalon.

Nor time, nor space gains precedence beyond
Where magical enchantment has increase;
For calmness reigns, as if some wondrous wand
Had charmed a world-that-was with lasting peace
Somewhere close to Avalon.

Familiar all shades in half-world's glow,
So many smiles extend a welcome cheer;
All yesterdays seem many years ago,
But still we'll find new trace of loves held dear,
Somewhere close to Avalon.

Some force within clear consciousness invites
Eternity that skirts this passing scene;
Angelic voices fill the distant heights,
Till memory remains what might have been
Somewhere close to Avalon.

# SONNET FOR ETERNITY

I too have been a lover of the Earth
And all its wonders.  All I've ever known
Has been a revelation; time has shown
That seasoned joys have everlasting worth.
The sun has smiled upon me, Heaven's mirth
Has laughed in thunder.  I have not outgrown
This patch of time; these treasures that I own
Are sky-borne days, a legacy from birth.

I fear not autumn, nor the fall of leaves,
Nor aging bones, nor body taxed with years;
Death's dart shall not deter me.  Life achieves
Infinity.  Beyond this span appears
A dream that's mine; my spirit has unfurled
Its certainty within a changing world.

# ENIGMA

Mercurial as an autumn wind,
his gust stirred leaves
of parted shades
through boughs of balmed
remembrance;
and thoughts, like birds,
took instant flight
across stilled worlds of
harmony.
We stemmed the gale of his advance
with candour culled from passive smiles,
and traced old ways
through common ground
to blend of sunlit
moments ...

but like some
migratory soul,
he rose upon a half-chance spell,
winging far from seasoned claims;
out beyond a dream once shared,
to heights of fading
       nimbus.

# SONNET - TO THE MOON SO BEAUTIFUL

Moon of cremola, in deep yoghurt skies,
Whisked from vanilla of crystalline stars,
Sweet falls the evening; your mixture belies
The dark bowl that bears you in the night's bars.
Around you, thick cloudings of blackcurrant jam,
And milk of spilt promise to moisten your shoon.
If I might consume you, my mouth would I cram,
But, like lapped cremola, you vanish too soon.

Could I but change you to low-fat cream cheese,
All poured upon night in heavenly spread,
The skies would be moonless; then at my ease,
Your smile would be plastered all over my bread!
Ah, custard of Cupid, some mouth-watered force
Decreed your selection for day's second course.

## ARRIVAL OF THE MUSE

Sometimes
out of cold winds,
sunlight,
sting of driven rain,
you come;
and come what will
or what you may
(or what you may not)
try to say,
- - - you come.

Your strange
abstraction is upon me;
clings to me and sings.
- - - Then should I
dwell upon my welcomings of you,
or bring you to prolonged delay,
and speak of you in this-wise?

      "It was this way,
      in driven rain,
      my muse arrived and we conferred,
      digressed, concurred;
      - - - made poetry, today,
      but not in words,
      but not in words!"

What would the neighbours say?

# TO A SPIDER

- on finding him languishing in the bath.

Bold creepy-crawly, there's no doubt
The bathroom clears when you're about,
Though progress up the waterspout
We must applaud.
How did you manage when, throughout,
Flushed waters poured?

Brief monster, card and glass will save
Your scuttles from a watery grave;
A just reward for one so brave,
Let's all agree.
Then shall our loved-ones horror waive
To set you free.

Behind the skirting, make your home,
Feel free to ponder, and to roam
Across the ceiling's lofty dome,
Where you shall reign.
Far better there than in the foam
Of some foul drain

# NIGHT SHADES

Between the ghosts of shivered trees crawls night,
And haunted owls are phantoms in the park.
The street-lamp's beam reveals the cat, and dark
Steals filigrees of moon from silvered flight.
Now creep half-shaped and shadowed things to sight
Where back-roads blunder back. The house-dogs bark
Upon a world where fear has left its mark,
In moments fading essence of delight.

This day we reckoned real is but a dream,
Where hope, itself, must wait upon the dawn
To shake the course of sleep with wakeful breath.
Our changing world is not what it may seem,
For Time that's yet to be is still unborn,
And curtained is the fall of night, this death.

# QUAYSIDE SUNDAY MARKET

Suddenly, below the hill,
a trestled fairground
sprawls across the Quay
beside the brooding waters,
buoyant to the cries,
not of gulls, but men
whose song is selling
socks, or fruit, or anything that goes,
in trailing pools of merchandise,
to lure those gathered there.

 - Not insects, but the shifting
crowds of folk, who watch
above a river teased with rain.
For who will buy?

And who will buy the towelled packs
from cheap-jack stands,
or cut-priced tools beside the bridge?
And who will seek the baubled deals
they bric-a-brac in plastic bags?

The morning brings the Bean-man
trayed with capsuled tricks,
the stone-faced policemen, two by two,
the busy tradesmen, selling
hardware, software,
anything you care to wear.

And still they come,
the old, the young,
a happy, rolling, boisterous crowd,
while folk, like crabs,
cram alleyways
to glutton on their spoils,
and harbingers of Hot Dogs
waft back the Sabbath
with indifferent breath.

## SONNET FOR THE LUCKY FISH (A LOCAL JUNK SHOP)

Beneath a garish sign their wares are spread,
And boxes spill late spoils into the street
Where, out of time, to pause time's passing feet,
Once-treasured gifts that erstwhile folk have shed,
Invite appraising gaze. The thoughtful thread
Past bric-a-brac and scattered tools to treat
Themselves to bargain-buys within, and greet
With joy some gem to take another's stead.

Thus, trinkets, books and simple well-loved things
Can often rouse the shades of former days;
And life moves on, while friendly token stays
(though second-hand) and to the moment clings.
 - A pleasure, then, to find this shop, for here
   We may yet reach the dreams of yesteryear.

# IN A KENTISH WORLD

When I came down by Appledore,
the land was green with spring;
broad skies beamed down from buttermilk,
and curlew on the wing
cried echoed joy to scattered fold,
as morning stirred the sheep.

- A simple glory to behold,
where dyke and hedgerow keep
the counterpane of former days
for time's untroubled fleece
of angels, white and Romney reared,
in patchwork fields at peace.

When I came down to Romney Town,
a host of silvern stars
lit lanterns on a drowsy world;
night's pearls peeped from the bars
of sandflats raising loitered birds,
whose shades to twilight cling.

I watched moon's shawl
drape Dymchurch Wall
 - and heard the shallows sing.

# IN A CINQUE-PORT TOWN

On seaward edge of Kentish shire,
By field and farm and telegraph wire,
This ancient town, beneath a sky
Where curlew wheel and dunlin fly,
Sleeps on beyond the boom and bell
Of dangerous tides once known so well;

But leaning cotts and winding street
Still echo to the constant feet
Of farmer, smuggler, fisherman, spy,
Or mantled stranger riding by
On steaming horse,
- - in search of rest,
With gold, for grog at his behest.

Still creaks the inn:
Each room and rafter
Trembling low with haunted laughter;
Voices raised from nights long-past,
Of farm-folk, men before-the-mast
And miller who, with different sail,
Anticipated western gale.

And in the churchyard, stone on stone
Tells of a land where time has flown.
Long-gone the seaman, yeoman, squire,
The plough-hand and the cattle-buyer,
All have died and are no more - - -

-- But when the rolling tide's ashore,
On such a night, when moon's aglow
And whistled wind beats to and fro,
You'll hear the fall of well-shod feet
As murmured shades slip down the street
To seek an inn.
Their course is clear - -
                          - - Though they've been gone
                              - - Full many a year!

# IN A LANTERNED NIGHT

Tang of brine, a harsh wind blowing
Dusted gulls from out of sky;
Beyond the bars, a township looming
Nigh two hundred years gone by.

Barnacled beneath a scarp line,
Cluttered dwellings thread their light.
      - Shadows of a bygone harbour,
        Phantoms in a lanterned night.

Beaten sheets from trembled mastheads,
Wooden staithes by lapping shores,
Aching timbers, trade signs creaking;
Shuttered windows, warehouse doors.

Cobbled streets, their house-walls leaning,
Alleys reeking tar and slime;
Echoed mirth from hidden taverns.
      - Canny seaport lost in time.

# SKY-PATCH IN DECEMBER

Ice-blue, waning,
ocean sky
is silvered down to furze of trees,
cold islands fade,
and waxen seas
flush out a magpie, gilding flight.

With strange accord, as cruising by,
town's gasping traffic,
nose to tail,
is burnished on the homeward run.

To no avail, a syrup sun
gilds Neo-Gothic towered church
and daubs the lurch
of drunken crows.
  - For day is done

- - - and down it goes,
as down from blue to smouldered grey,
last bastion - - - a flaming ray,
smiles out upon a sickle moon.

# RHYMESTERS OF THE STRANDS

The riding lights have shed their gold
Beside a silver quay,
Where moonlight curls to gossamer
My white-sailed argosy.

A bold three-masted, square-rigged craft
On course for distant shore;
We'll weigh the anchor ere the dawn,
Lest fading time restore
Brief charm to dross of wasted scope,
And sail beyond the bars,
Till poesy finds wings of hope
Among the boundless stars.

We'll sail where new tomorrow brings
Great gems of lasting light,
As star-swept sings the universe
In magical delight.

My cargo is a sheaf of dreams
For trade in faery lands;
My crew are those whom fortune deems
The rhymesters of the strands.

For, in those heights, sweet minstrelsy
Awaits with lasting song,
- We'll sail beyond the moment's glow
To lands where we belong.

# WITHIN A POSTCARD WORLD

Out of the sands of morning,
Beyond the hour-glass,
I found within a moment's spell
A city street I knew quite well,
Yet time decreed I could not know
Their postcard world of yesterday.

Within that street I wound my way,
As time was from its moment shed
With footsteps frozen in their tread,
And shops along fate's darkened way
Were eerie in their stillness.

Antique cars were everywhere,
Gem-studded droplets decked the air,
Sparkling fashions (British Made)
On persons seen in time that's strayed;
Each waxen glance of joy or pain.
Unmoved within the spangled rain.

A bow-backed tram, no longer fleeting,
Stayed raised arm for Heaton's greeting,
Clinging to its web of thread.
  - I left the moment with its dead,
But wondered how such shades could pass
So far beyond the hour-glass.

# TO A POET A THOUSAND YEARS HENCE

God bless the sanguine soul who hears
The voice of a poet long since dead,
Imbued with purpose that endears,
For mine are the words that shall be read,
I who am dead a thousand years.

Remembrance rouses dreams among
Those days long past, but still remains,
Within a lasting minstrel throng,
The voice of one who shaped refrains
And wrote this sweet archaic song.

This world is not as it appears;
Existence feigns a changing face.
Though life is but a vale of tears,
I who spurned Death's cold embrace,
Send you my words for messengers.

My verses ever shall belong
To those aggrieved, to those oppressed,
That we might harmonise in song
Beyond life's shades I've laid to rest,
The way I shall not pass along.

# BALLADE OF BOLD RESOLVE

Our changing world shapes circumstance anew,
And vanquished years soon drift beyond recall;
Life's facets find fresh shades as time threads through
Dense forests of our days, where moments fall,
Till fate holds even chance within its thrawl.
Achievement is more sweet than passing fame.

Discerning souls may readily eschew
The baying praise of crowds where Babels sprawl.
Each monument that's raised to shape Man's due
In time becomes a worthless falderal,
And deeds that marred his days might then appal.
Integrity is deemed Man's finest aim;
Achievement is more sweet than passing fame.

All former hopes, and trusted friends we knew,
Must sadly fade down memory's dark hall;
Our days with dulled ambition we imbue,
But stroke of death no power may forestall.
What then, if brief success be praised by all;
Would dreams that life holds dear seem much the same?
        - Achievement is more sweet than passing fame.

While fame be but the province of the few,
Endeavours little known are blessed withall;
Then let us honour every heart that's true,
Whose talent shines, though praise of worth be small,
Lest inspiration spurned be turned to gall;
For, though the moment's man be praised by name,
Achievement is more sweet than passing fame.

# ELYSIUM

Too bright by far, nor may mortals see
Beyond Time's misted final veil;
Nor hear Death's wondrous minstrelsy,
And live to tell the tale.
Too bright by far, and yet must we come
    - - - - Elysium!

Turn but a wing, and chance but a flame,
Cling to the call of God-given name,
Thrill to the pulse of celestial drum,
    - - - - Elysium!

Vision supernal, sweet blossoming spring;
A timeless enchantment whose troubadours sing
From the soul of Joy's being,
Where calm zephyrs hum
Through the golden veiled groves of
    - - - - Elysium!

And we traverse the shades of a calm folding night,
Gusted through sapphire seas
Where the seraphs spread light,
To the heart of Life's dreams
In the Isles of The Blest,
Where peace is abounding
And souls are at rest;

Where mountains are kissed
With libations of wine,
And Arcady's lit with a dream that is mine;
For prophet and poet and minstrel must come
Beyond the last veil to Elysium.

Aye, too bright by far,
Yet there's glory for some
When destiny leads to
- - Elysium.

# LITANY OF PEACE

Like the silence on a hillside,
Like the sighing of a sigh,
Like the ripple of a fountain,
Like a mother's lullaby,
Like the balm of soughing woodland
When the storm has passed us by;
Like a birdsong bringing Peace.

Like a muslin veil on cities
When long day has filled its spell,
Like an old familiar story,
Like the smiles we know so well,
Like the lapping hush of breakers
When the sea has spent its swell;
Like a litany of Peace.

Like a moment of warm laughter
In the harmony of friends,
Like the healing of forgiveness
When a loved-one makes amends,
Like a welcome truth that lingers
In a world that never ends;
Like a lasting gift of Peace.

# MR SHAKESPEARE GOES SHOPPING

These fabled aisles, this bright emporium;
This temple raised for townsfolk, fit for kings,
To which e'en those of low estate may come;
This Presto pile - so filled with wondrous things!
Its spacious halls well-lit through marbled ways
Breathe zephyrs from glazed heights to cool a throng,
Where serried shelves and sweetmeats heaping trays
Bring myriad maids with baskets, ere not long.

Now see how scattered clans await tilled bells,
While hidden minstrels pipe incessant airs
O'er Mazes ruled by check queens - As each sells
To moment's souls that drift to far affairs.
But I, like Tantalus, am cursed by fate;
My choicest fruits are canned in armour plate.

# INCIDENT IN A NEWCASTLE CHURCH PORCH

"Mammy!" cried the child,
"That man - -
the one who has the teeth,
he says he likes my shoes!"
 - Mum's face had turned three shades of red
behind a plate-glass portico.

The overflow from Morning Mass
was interspersed with shuffled men
who manned the doorways,
bagged the brass,
and sorted out their Sunday plate,
oblivious to capers (as a rule)
of those arriving late:
the grim travails of mothered care,
and ones and twos of those who might
take flight before the final hymn.

But there it was again:
        "That man, that man,
        he likes my shoes;
        - - - the one who has the teeth.
          - That man!"

And punctured silence threatened prayer
where troubled bodies heaved beneath
the moment's new temptation.
Hysteria was in the air
as liturgy was shed
in pagan, shaking jollity.
        - "He likes my shoes!"
           he said.

# THE LIBRARY WILL BE CLOSING SOON

Out of damp and nagging
Rainfall of a mizzled night,
I came on neon straining light
Across a civic portico.
Several minutes yet to go
Before the brash attendant came,
Uniform upon his game
Of moving stragglers from the site.

Ten-to-eight. The library
Was sealing off its cosy nooks
Bedecked with posters and a spate
Of townsfolk clutching books.

And there she sat, forlorn, alone,
A moulding cast from life-impaired;
I found her, hunched upon a seat,
Banana skins around her feet.
            - An artefact of stone.

Grey coat,
Grey face, grey eyes that stared
Into the cracks of haunted years;
And waxen spears of tangled hair
That dangled from a face once fair
To shadows all her own.
A wretch forsaken, clad in rags,
Her worthless world in plastic bags.

Five-to-eight.  The library
Was making fast its drawers and doors;
While homesped flotsam marked her plight,
Shrugged once for God,
And passed into the night.

I sat beside her, tried to talk
To reassure her, tried to say,
        "If only I could help some way,
        Some help, perhaps a little token?"
Hoped she wouldn't mind I'd spoken.
- Would not mind.

The peak-capped man,
The people left behind
Were torn
Between amusement and a show of scorn.

Eight O-Clock.  The library
Extinguished light.
I pressed some money to her hand,
Hoping that she'd understand.
Grey eyes she raised - a look of pain,
And then the night,
The slow and sobbing
        Rain.

# FIRST-ELECTED ANIMAL-RIGHTS
# INDEPENDENT M.P.

No-one was quite certain
how his name had first
occurred upon the list.
In vain did candidates insist
the whole thing was absurd
and never had been known before;
for if, when time had come to pass
and all the world had heard
our next M.P. would be an ass,
what then would lie in store?

The Tory bloke was furious;
declared the whole thing spurious.
The Liberal Alliance
twittered in defiance,
and Labour was bereft.
  - Their candidate moved swiftly to the Left!

Well, there it was at last,
no more than we'd suspected;
When finally the votes were cast
and ballot tins collected
  - Recriminations, accusations!
A donkey by the name of Bray,
an Independent Ass (they say),
had duly been elected.

# ENGLAND'S CAUSE

Those tattered flags, those emblems of lost days,
Bestrewn through silent churches of the land;
Those monuments of war, whereon we gaze
 - Those martial airs, so poignant and so grand;
Those anthems raised to praise a nation's might;
Those ships we sailed by many foreign shores;
Those men who bled for freedom, in the fight
To save our sovereign state and England's cause;

Are they to be forgotten, like a dream,
Or something that occurred by merest chance?
Did those who fought so bravely not redeem
A nation's pride from enemy advance?
    - Those men who died for England died in vain
    If England's loss becomes another's gain!

# TO A HIDDEN BIRD

It seemed as if a thousand sparks enflamed
An interlacing canopy of green,
Till gold and silver glittered strands were seen
In tapestry that sunlight had proclaimed;
Then softly, though by quietude untamed,
Where brightest leaves shone glory in the Dene,
Cascades of rippled music came between
Untrodden groves, from singer yet unnamed.

For out of flame, there sang the hidden bird,
A plaintive minstrel, piping through the boughs
With more than normal eloquence allows;
So beautiful a song I'd seldom heard.
My soul was charmed by this most welcome host,
But nowhere could I trace the moment's ghost.

# TO AUTUMN

The garden's lit so like a theatre stage,
With back-cloth dwellings etched on sheeted blue;
Footlights of sun raise autumn's phase anew
And breezes from the wings strained boughs assuage.
All sound is stilled that motion might engage
In dancing flame, fine leaves of varied hue
Down shifting cluttered ways, where must ensue
Late curtain-calls till wintry winds shall rage.

Arrives the robin - prologue to the show,
With charm of mime (though later how he sings!)
The magpie struts his course, so too the crow
- - - Till soon this sunlit patch is graced with birds
To improvise a plot that needs no words
But ritual, and all the season brings.

# THE HERITAGE

And was it, then, from faded sounds
o'er moss-spread, undulating mounds,
that raised their cold
remembrance
from the ruined stones of Time;
or was it from some might-have-been
we'd sensed the martial glory
of an empire past its prime
   - timeless as the curlew's call?
- - You know this was not all,
for did we not then feel
lost moments shared together,
quickening a glint of steel
and booted scrape of leather
on the Wall,
as out of clambered images
emergent sunlight made that leap
to martial ranks of Romans,
from the settled world we keep?

# ON PENSHAW HILL

For no apparent reason, on a hill,
Irresolute,majestic and half-mad,
This blackened colonnade remains,
Stately,
Like some ancient king
Stilled into paralysis.

And nothing stirs this settled spell
But whispered winds that prey,
Prying every whichway,
As the sun
Sharpens its quick tumblers over stone.

Overhead, black ravens rise,
Fanning watchful flight,
While those who climb the mound to see,
Can only pause to ponder
What might have been, and why:
 - This object of Masonic pride,
Etched and columned,
Set upon a hill
In sad remembrance of a might
That never was.

# WAITING FOR MARGARET

Straight down the polished corridor,
As far as you can go;
Turn left, then left,
Then left again.
Most outpatients will know
Location of Reception Desk,
If unsure of the way.
There's seats there, in the waiting-room,
Within an offshoot bay.

Offshoot bay, all vinyl-tiled,
Emulsioned purple-grey;
My wife, ensconsed in treatment room,
Requests that here I stay,
To stare at frosted window screen
That covers half a wall.
 - No newspaper, no magazine,
Just empty chairs, that's all.

Sound of footsteps on the stairs,
Clipped voices echoed low,
And squeaking doors, till time restores
The murmured, measured flow
Of air-conditioned, drowsing drone.
A trolley trundles by;
Metallic clicks, a whirr of feet,
More voices - - - -


Heave a sigh,
Alone within a waiting-room;
Strange hubbub fills the air.
This world's replete with clattered feet
- - - - - And waiting's hard to bear.

# A NIGHT FOR THE CATS

Mesmerised by moonlight
in the calm of brief estate,
by straggled hedge and shadowed wall,
within the street-lamp's ambered shawl,
cats luxuriate.

Their lethargy stays loosened limbs
with feline furred mendacity,
but flight strikes diamonds
in their eyes,
as footsteps, rousing sharp surprise,
carve echoes where,
within their world,
they keep a sense of ritual.

And watching from night's dim retreats
they brood on favoured
vantage points;
or, with cacophonous refrain,
cry out from tiers of terraced streets,
or cross our paths with catgut song,
subservient with fawnings feigned,
till wildness cautions.

Cats belong
to darkened plots of deep disdain,
where moonlight, cold and driven rain
rake lost primaeval
jungles.

# BEYOND THE BRIDGE

Within the oldest quarter of the town,
Where once Time's huddled craft berthed by the Quay,
Unhurried Sunday seekers saunter down
For bargains and rare merchandise. - Now see
Those tented booths, the cheapjacks and their wares,
The job-lot touts who charm with choicest phrase,
Oblivious to scorn and chancing stares,
Where morning smiles and church observance strays.

To bide thereby, where time and fancy dwell,
Some ritual divines that folk must go
Where grey gull wheels its wide and weaving spell,
And tryst is kept with slumbered Tyne below.
        - Here, once a week, those constant shoals pass by
        Beyond the bridge - - - beneath a sabbath sky.

# WAR MEMORIAL - BARRASS BRIDGE (NEWCASTLE UPON TYNE)

Men of monumental mettle,
marching into history and death.
 - How quickly we forget them,
we of peerless progeny;
how readily we pass them by,
their stark, unyielding gallantry
marshalled to the Call.
And yet - - - how calm, how beautiful!
Some craftsman has with skill portrayed
a vision cast from timelessness,
tracing courage, carving pride
where loyal limbs still stiffen
to their last adieu.

Beyond them, bright, young smiling girls,
radiant from sandwich queues,
have left their shops and office blocks
to seek their finest hour;
while, hard by this memorial,
Time's cocksure youth - tomorrow's men,
with little care for history,
stride out into their afternoon
to flaunt the world with denim
in a war of Let's Pretend.

# BESSIE SURTEES - BALLAD

The urchins danced like merry hell,
And pennies splashed like rain
As, through the town
In mayoral gown,
Sir Walter Blackett came.
    - Six chestnut mares to pull his coach,
    Four footmen, servants three,
    And fifteen lads with crimson cloaks
    For all the world to see.

To latticed windows down The Side
Young wives and maidens strayed,
Till soon they caught
The sun-shot gold
His gilded carriage sprayed.
    - An aging knight, five times a mayor,
    Whose wish was but to wed;
    And richest in the canny town,
    When all was done and said.

When all was done and said, he came
To barter for the hand
Of lovely Bessie Surtees
- Aye, the fairest in the land.
Great gifts he brought, and jewelled rings
That none might say him nay;
Fine clothes to wear,
And servant maids
If she'd but name the day.
If she'd but name the day, he said,

She'd wear a velvet gown.
A castle in the country
And a house in London Town
Would be the least that he could give.
Yea, more than that he'd do,
If only she would be his wife.
- His love for her was true.

His love for her was true, he said.
T'was whispered time again
By townsfolk up and down the chares
Till soon, along Love Lane,
T'was whispered, aye, with many a wink
(By those who knew him well)
To Johnny Scott, the coalman's son,
Who loved the Quayside belle.

When first they whispered him the news
His broad face raised a grin;
He roared with laughter,
Clapped his side
And cried, "T'would be a sin
To strike Sir Walter Blackett down,
And surely she'll say nay;
For all his lands and gilded coach,
She'll send the man away."

The next news that they whispered him
John's smile was grim and cold;
Old Surtees had betrayed his lass
For the sake of yellow gold.
For the sake of yellow gold, they said
(T'was whispered down the lane)

She'll marry old Sir Walter,
And he'd ne'er see her again.

In the shadowy town when the moon was down
One cold November night,
When even the cats,
The rats and the bats
Had seldom appeared in sight,
And the night-watch huddled in corner coves
Awaiting the new morn's glow,
There rattled a casement down The Side
 - And a ladder appeared below.

Aye, a ladder appeared below the house
Where Aubone Surtees dwelt.
In the dead of the night,
By candle-light,
The lass at the casement felt
It was time to leave,
Though she wept on the sleeve
Of her rich and comely gown;
But her John was below
And t'was time to go
        - So out of the window and down.

Aye, out of the window, and down she sped
As he held the ladder still,
And her foot to each rung
Was a feeling so sweet,
But her young heart sensed that thrill
Of fear, lest the dogs
Or the neighbours should wake
And peer from their casements on high

On those who would lark
With their ladders, by dark.
      - Ah, t'would raise such a hue and a cry.

And t'would raise such a hue and a cry to learn,
When the sun loomed high in the east,
That his daughter was gone
With the coal-man's son
To deny them their wedding feast.
Aye, the maids gave alarm
When they found that a-bed
No mistress, no Bessie was there.
Like a thief in the night
She had taken to flight
With her love - - - in a carriage and pair.

And the urchins danced like merry hell,
The pennies splashed like rain
As through the town, in mayoral gown,
Old Blackett, once again,
With six brown mares,
A gilded coach,
And men in livery,
Came down The Side to claim his bride
      - her husband for to be.

And the urchins danced like merry hell,
And loud laughed everyone,
Except Pa-pa and the eldern knight.
      - She had gone with the coalman's son.

# THE TYNE BRIDGE

Astride a heaving river, high
above the stack-lines of the wharves,
there dwells a rainbow,
rivetted in steel,
majestic, haunched and skeletal.
An archway of the day, it spans
a single stretch of thoroughfare
to scape dark, brooding
waters of the Tyne.

The dinosaur is fretted green,
familiar its timeless form,
yet strangely styled
in marked and metalled
curvature of poise.

Yet more than this;
To those who care,
this gateway of the North remains
a monument to industry,
a settlement, a fond bequest.
 - Reminder of a shirt-sleeved brag
that gave the world a bridge

# A PILGRIM STREET BALLAD

If you likes your bit o'peace,
There's a job there in the police,
Or you might become a soldier for a spell,
But when it's fightin' fires
You will run like 'lectric wires,
And pull your pumpin'
Hoses half-to-hell.

    Chorus
        Then it's:
           "Quick, lads, at the double;
           There's a call-out."
        That means trouble,
And you'll get no sleep throughout the flamin' night!
Aye, there's no time for your supper,
Or that little extra cuppa,
When the bells go down
And somewhere's all alight.

Now the lads doon Pilgrim Street
Are accustomed to the heat.
- They can tackle blazes burning to the sky.
And great feelings they arouse
When they rescue stranded cows,
Or when their polished tender travels by.

When it comes to fireman's drill,
There is always time to kill
(Or someone else) when practising below.
And their ladders SELDOM fall
When they're propped against the wall
While the firemen play their hoses
To and fro.

There's a lad there, name o' DANCER,
Who will often take a chance, sir,
When it comes to raising laughter in the Mess;
And there's many knows the score,
With their boots screwed to the floor.
- If they don't know who's done it,
They can guess.

Then there's PURVIS, who's a bouncer
(On his nights off) down the town, sir,
With commitments that would turn your hair to grey;
For he's workin' ev'ry night, sir;
Always ready for a fight, sir,
With a mortgage and a hundred bills to pay.

With the minimum of fuss
They can overtake a bus,
Or make a one-way street run either way;
And their engine's often seen
Chasin' cyclists between
Newcastle and the road to Whitley Bay.

Aye, they've saved a blazin' pub,
Stopped a restaurant toastin' grub,
And washed away a thousand smoking cars.
In a host of burnt retreats
You may find them doon the streets
As they pose in yellow helmets
'Neath the stars.

And the townsfolk think they're great,
Though the tender's sometimes late
If they've had a spot o' curry for their teas;
And when running round with hoses
They don't stop to blow their noses.
      - Apart from which, the fireman's sure to please.

    Chorus
        Then it's:
            "Quick, lads, at the double;
            There's a call-out."
        That means trouble,
And you'll get no sleep throughout the flamin' night!
Aye, there's no time for your supper,
Or that little extra cuppa,
When the bells go down
And somewhere's all alight.

# ROMAN FORT (HADRIAN'S WALL)

We found the Fort of Housesteads
On hummockings of hills,
Fragmenting paths
Where spears of grass
Spiked nettles in the rills,
And buttercups in scheming clans
Laid siege to martial mound.

Perhaps it was the sound
Of sheep lamenting
Dry-stone fold,
Or waverings
Where hayfields stirred the mould,
Soughing on the new-mown
Wisps, now warm
With bake of dung
That clung
To days more meaningful than these.

The heat-haze had its way
With Granary, Praetorium
And other lumps of grey.
- Then... Out across the sprawling ridge,
Time's sentinels of stone.

# BALLAD FOR THE TYNE

You men of paper politics,
You lords of high degree,
Have you gazed upon the slipways,
Seen the ships we've put to sea?
Or wandered down the wharf-sides, Sirs,
Beyond the clang of steel,
And watched the restless waters swell,
The river gulls that wheel
From wake of e'en the smallest craft
To proud ships of the line?
      - Then think again
      You paper men,
      This is the River Tyne.

            Aye, we built the Mauretania,
            The monarchs of the waves;
            We fitted out your fighting-ships
            And saved from salty graves
            A host of battered merchantmen,
            Our nation for to serve;
            But now the shipyards face neglect.
            - Is this what we deserve?

What price the finest of the line,
Four-funnelled, proud and free:
The great Superb, the Nelson;
Aye,
The Empress - on the lee,
The Gripsholme and the Hector

And the noble Northern Star?
And would you ask who built these ships?
    - The world knows who we are.

You men of paper politics,
Our lads have served you well;
In times of peace and war they've patched
More craft than words can tell.
Our yards are now on harder times,
But lest you might forget,
The skills are here to build in steel
The finest vessels yet.

        For we built the Mauretania,
        The monarchs of the waves;
        We fitted out your fighting-ships
        And saved from salty graves
        A host of battered merchantmen,
        Our nation for to serve;
        But now the shipyards face neglect.
           - Is this what we deserve?

# SHIPS BY THE QUAY

So often I've wandered by Newcastle Quayside,
And long have I pondered this strange myster-ee:
Fine buildings abound there,
And townsfolk are thriving,
But where are the ships sailing home from sea?

    CHORUS   And where are the Jack-Tars,
                  The stevedores, the carters,
                  The waggoners cursing - - wherever they be;
                  The clatter of barrels,
                  The tumbledown boxes;
                  And where are the sailor-lads
                  Home from the sea?

Aye, once there were vessels from deep distant waters,
Fine craft with their mastheads as tall as a tree;
Then came the steamers,
And boats built for dreamers,
But gone are the sailors who put out to sea.

    CHORUS   And where are the Jack-Tars,
                  The stevedores, the carters,
                  The waggoners cursing - - wherever they be;
                  The clatter of barrels,
                  The tumbledown boxes;
                  And where are the sailor-lads
                  Home from the sea?

And sometimes I find through the mist of my dreaming,
This canny old seaport as life used to be.
          - If gold could provide it,
          Old heads would be scheming
To fill the Tyne's moorings with ships by the Quay.

          CHORUS   And where are the Jack-Tars,
                   The stevedores, the carters,
                   The waggoners cursing - - wherever they be;
                   The clatter of barrels,
                   The tumbledown boxes;
                   And where are the sailor-lads
                   Home from the sea?

Oh, the dark rippled waters are heaving and brawling,
And down swoop the gulls where the river runs free;
But silent the foghorns - -
No more shall we hear them,
Their brazen tones calling
When home from the sea.

          CHORUS   And where are the Jack-Tars,
                   The stevedores, the carters,
                   The waggoners cursing - - wherever they be;
                   The clatter of barrels,
                   The tumbledown boxes;
                   And where are the sailor-lads
                   Home from the sea?

# THE MERMAID

I found her by the seashore
In a rock-strewn sweep of bay,
Where fury of the foaming tides
Lashed time-worn cliffs of grey.

So ghostly, yet so beautiful,
Bright seaweed graced her hair,
That hung in ringlets to her waist;
She was a maiden fair!

Her body glistened in the spray,
And haunting was her sigh;
Grey seabirds wheeled around her head
With savage echoed cry.

Quick sunlight sparkled sequin gems
From green and silvered tail.
Her eyes were fixed upon me, then;
Her cheeks so deathly pale.

As rearing waves leapt to the land,
Her sigh was like the sea.
She smiled. The wind brushed through her hair;
And still she gazed on me.

"Oh, windswept man, with beard so white,
What brings you here?" cried she.
"And have you sailed the ocean foam
That is so wild and free?
And will you save me from my fate?
        - Forever must I roam

In bounden thrall to fearsome tides
Beneath the sky's wide dome.

But if a soul might care for me,
That spell shall surely break,
For stronger is the bond of love
Than all the sea might take!
  - So, save me from this wind-cursed life,
And I'll be true to thee!"

I stood entranced, through time and tide,
Strange sound had filled the air.
Quick sunlight danced within her eyes
And burnished gold her hair.

She stirred, and raised her slender arms,
As waves crashed round her still.
I longed to wade to hold her close,
But could not find the will.

Rough surf became a seething squall;
Grey seabirds swept the sky.
Dark storm clouds burst upon the bay
  - And then - - - that parting sigh!

My mermaid she was gone from me.
I heard her fading song:
              " In restless tides I'll seek my dreams,
              For here's where I belong.
              And here's where I belong," wailed she,
              " And here's where I belong.
              In restless tides I'll seek my dreams,
              For here's where I belong - - - "

# HARBOUR LIGHTS

A stretch beyond the Ferry Stage,
Towards Low Lights, the Quay
Spread moonshine through the darkness;
For night's tranquillity
Had settled on this old Tyne port
Where fishing boats at rest,
And circlings of hungry gulls
Were numbered with the blest;
While out upon the hidden bars
Late streams of lamplit gold
Spilled scattered strands across the Tyne
     - A beauty to behold!
And joy it was to trace that gleam
Along the southern shore,
Where lights shone down
From South Shields town
(As oft in times before),
Whose clustered dwellings, on those banks,
With white facades were seen;
And shore to shore a strange allure
Where all was calm between.
It brought a sense of former days,
And this I tell you true,
Of all the wonders of the night,
There is no finer view.

# IN AUTUMN DAYS

Rare candour stirs the instance of her smile,
So radiant those eyes with starlight glow;
Her constant charms my very soul beguile.
 - I'd give my all, my fervent love to show.

So radiant those eyes with starlight glow,
Her words are like the ripples of a stream;
I'd give my all, my fervent love to show,
But youth has passed; no spell may time redeem,

How through my vale of days she's shaped life's course;
Of joy and sadness we have had our share,
And yet, kind fate shall not embrace remorse,
For nothing may our source of love impair.

Of joy and sadness we have had our share;
Cloud gatherings of grief have passed us by,
For nothing may our source of love impair
In autumn days that linger with a sigh.

Cloud gatherings of grief have passed us by,
And though hard times might face us once again
In autumn days that linger with a sigh,
Her starlight glow still nurtures love's refrain.

And though hard times might face us once again,
Together we shall walk that extra mile.
Her starlight glow still nurtures love's refrain;
Rare candour stirs the instance of her smile.

## SIMPLY THIS

I have seen the fiery sun set
in a multilucent sky,
gleaned the dawn from silvern ashes in the east;
I have wandered by sea breakers,
felt its feathered surf flow by;
sought the rivered falls whose torrents never cease.

I have traced greened earth before me
in a counterpane of fields,
and climbed the craggy rocks, the highest hill,
I have marvelled at creation,
smiled on all that Nature yields;
I have sipped from life, yet never had my fill.

Near the little hamlets sleeping
in the lands of yesterday,
I have wandered through the long grass in the vales,
where the sun has burst on summer,
winter's snow, the flowered May,
and leafy woodlands beating autumn trails.

Yet I've loved the city sky-lines,
savoured roof tops dark with dew;
marked the lazy river overhung with cranes.
I have walked the streets at midnight,
watched the shadowed world anew
casting gems of moonlight, cobbled down the lanes.

And these simple gifts I've gathered
down the passing of the years,
though it matters not my song may meet with scorn.
With my wondrous world around me
what care I if no-one shares
these treasures?
I thank God that I was born.

# A GREATER GOLD

My song is not of palaced kings
Carriaged in pomp for rare delight,
Nor of bold war, nor martial things
whose wrongs uphold the cause of Right.

Ambition's dizzy heights shall sway
No pride in me; I shall not pine
For shades beyond this passing clay,
Deserting dreams and what is mine.

Though friendship's cup be frothed with ale,
I would not seek the tavern's glow.
Aye, feasting might the world regale
With richest fare - But I'd not go,

For I belong to quiet span
Whose life extends through simple ways,
Where never prize was greater than
The treasured weft of homespun days.

So I'll not yearn for high estate,
With power's rod and wealth untold,
Nor morsels from the hand of fate,
For I have found - - - a greater gold.

Bernard M. Jackson, a retired teacher, has for many years been prominent as a poet and review writer in the small press poetry scene of the UK and India. A number of his poems and reviews have also been extensively featured in various poetry magazines in the U.S.A., Greece, Australia and Korea.

He is an honoured member of CINQUE PORTS POETS (England), and has been accorded membership of the INTERNATIONAL ASSOCIATION of WRITERS and ARTISTS (Blufton - Ohio, U.S.A.). His poems have been published in THIS ENGLAND and EVERGREEN magazine, besides being included in POETS ENGLAND (Norfolk Anthology) and quite a number of UK anthologies and magazines. Besides being the chief review writer for REACH POETRY, he is Articles Writer for the QUANTUM LEAP magazine and current POETRY ADVISOR to Norfolk Poets and Writers. His work in India is rather more widespread. He is UK Advisor to METVERSE MUSE (Visakhapatnam), Advisory Panel Member of POETCRIT (Maranda - India), Associate Assistant-Editor of Poets India International and established Review Writer for BRIDGE-IN-MAKING, CANOPY, and VOICE OF KOLKATA (Calcutta) magazines. Within the UK many of his featured articles have been published by POETIC HOURS (Nottingham) and have regularly appeared in WRITERS' FORUM Magazine. His previously published collections include A FEATHER FOR YOUR THOUGHTS * * NOW YOU HAS JAZZ * * A SEASON'S GOLD * * BALLADS OF A NORTHERN TOWN * * A LEEDS CHILDHOOD, each of which is available from the author.

B.M.J., as he is popularly known, is the proud recipient of a Gold Medallion award for services to poetry, together with FELLOWSHIP of the TEMPLE of ARTS ACADEMY, based in New Zealand.

**Indigo Dreams Publishing**
**132 Hinckley Road**
**Stoney Stanton**
**Leicestershire**
**LE9 4LN**
**www.indigodreams.co.uk**